MW01119410

Secrets
to a
HAPPY LIFE

From a dog named Reilly

As told to
Bill Curley

ISBN: 978-1-4834-5570-9 (sc)
ISBN: 978-1-4834-5571-6 (e)

Lulu Publishing Services rev. date: 03/09/2017

Acknowledgements

Reilly and I are both blessed to have the love of my soulmate, Diane, who brings happiness and support to both our lives every single day. Thanks are also due to the following people who gave generously of their time and enthusiasm. Gary Gray, my creative mentor. Bryon De France who took the time out of his very busy life to give me insight into the perspective and motivation of a mind unburdened by human ego, pride, anger, and regret. Leslie Cole for her advice on graphics. Kinga Malinowski who gave some of her valuable time in the search for the perfect photo of Reilly. Mary Dwan King who took the lovely rear cover shot of Reilly telling me some of his secrets. Christine Green who took the wonderful cover photo of Reilly. Lastly, to Barbara Cowles, a truly gentle soul whose deep love and understanding of our canine companions was a beacon to follow.

Bill's Prologue

Reilly is my dog. He is a 75-pound, apricot colored, standard poodle. I think he's quite handsome, but I'm probably a bit biased. He's also very smart and very gentle. He has brought love and joy to the life of my wife, Diane, and I.

His most striking characteristic is that he is always happy. Of course, most dogs are a lot happier than their human masters. I'm convinced that if there was ever such a thing as a canine theme song, it would be, "Don't worry. Be happy." With that said, I honestly believe Reilly is exceptionally happy, even for a dog. Every day, every hour, every minute seems to bring him great pleasure.

When Diane and I first saw him at the breeder's kennel, his littermates hurled themselves at the gate in frenzied anticipation of a treat or a pat. Reilly, on the other hand, sat quietly in the rear of the pen calmly looking at us.

We asked to hold him and he made himself comfortable in our laps. He showed no fear of these two giant strangers. He won my heart when he looked up at me and licked my arm. I asked the breeder if his calm, laid-back behavior was normal. She told us that occasionally there is a pup like him in some litters. She calls them "monks" or "thinkers".

Unlike their brothers and sisters, such dogs think before they act. They don't do things just because they can. They do them because they want to … because they make them happy. Reilly has proved to be a thinker and his choices always seem to please him.

I have wondered about this ever since we brought him home. To satisfy my curiosity I recently sat down with him and asked him why he was so doggone happy. Our conversations occurred over several days and I transcribed all of Reilly's wise words verbatim. When I was done, I knew I had to share his thoughts with others. They just make so much sense.

I hope you find these "secrets" as instructive and enlightening as I did. I've also included relevant quotations about the various subjects Reilly addresses as well as quotations about dogs, their outlook on life, and their relationships with their human family.

Bill

Quotations

"If you don't own a dog, at least one, there is not necessarily anything wrong with you, but there may be something wrong with your life."
Roger Caras

"A dog is not 'almost human' and I know of no greater insult to the canine race than to describe it as such."
John Holmes

Reilly's Prologue

I had mixed feelings when Bill told me he wanted to sit down and find out why I'm always happy. I wasn't thrilled at the prospect of spending hours discussing the obvious. I'd rather be playing with a chew toy, running around the yard, or just sleeping. We dogs aren't a very philosophical bunch.

But Bill seemed really set on the idea and I do love the big guy. Of far greater importance is the fact that he's the one who buys the chow and the chew toys. I don't have a clue where to buy dog food or how to pay for it so I have to humor the man.

What I've tried to do here is tell you why I do what I do and explain why it makes me happy. Remember, just as with every dog, it's all about me. I don't claim to speak for great Danes, Chihuahuas, or even other standard poodles. These mental droppings are my poop alone.

I've also tried to explain how you human folk might benefit from having the same outlook on life. You may think some of these "secrets" are a bit unusual. So what? You've got nothing to lose by giving them a try. You may also disagree with some of them. That's your prerogative.

Something else I should point out is that I'm no rocket scientist. My educational background is limited to a few obedience classes. You're not going to get any complex, intellectual insights here. Everything I have to say is pretty simple.

Bill has read me the final draft. If you think that the original discussion with him was boring for me, you can't imagine how excruciating it was to have it regurgitated back to me. It was almost enough to make me, well, regurgitate.

Anyhow, my job is done and I can go back to being a dog. I hope for Bill's sake you get something out of my ramblings. If not, it's no skin off my big wet nose. Talk to Bill.

Reilly

Quotations

"I used to look at (my dog) Smokey and think, 'If you were a little smarter, you could tell me what you were thinking' and he'd look at me like he was saying, 'If you were a little smarter, I wouldn't have to.'"
Fred Jungclaus

"Dogs can talk. You just have to know how to listen."
Barbara Cowles

"Dogs are not our whole life, but they make our lives whole."
Roger Caras

44 Secrets to a Happy Life

1

Live in the present

Reilly began, "Life is really simple, Bill. You humans just complicate it with irrelevant stuff. The only true reality is the present moment. I would hate to own a watch. I'm only interested in one time … NOW. The past is over so why think about it? The future is just a fiction until it becomes the present. Life becomes simple once you grasp this concept.

"Unfortunately, you humans are too easily distracted from the present moment. A dog doesn't worry about what he did the day before or how he can get better at it tomorrow. We put all our energy and being into the present. If you take nothing else away from what I have to say, recognize this simple truth and concentrate on living in the present."

It is a simple concept and I find it easy to accept intellectually. The difficulty lies in living it.

Quotations

"You can always cope with the present moment, but you cannot cope with something that is only a mind projection — you cannot cope with the future or recreate the past."
Eckhart Tolle,
Practicing The Power Of Now

"Life can be found only in the present moment. The past is gone, the future is not yet here, and if we do not go back to ourselves in the present moment, we cannot be in touch with life."
Thich Nhat Hanh

"The secret of health for both mind and body is not to mourn for the past, worry about the future, or anticipate troubles, but to live in the present moment wisely and earnestly."
Buddha

"Today is a most unusual day, because we have never lived it before; we will never live it again. It is the only day we have."
William Arthur Ward

"There are two days in the week about which and upon which I never worry ... yesterday and tomorrow."
Robert Jones Burdette

2

Smell the "roses"

"Why do you always sniff everything and everyone?" I asked.

He gave me a goofy grin. "Because I can, my friend. You see smell is my most powerful sense. Your nose can't smell even a fraction of the things mine can."

I nodded in agreement. "I read somewhere that a dog's sense of smell might be thousands of times more sensitive than a human's."

Reilly agreed. "Sounds about right. That's why I've never encountered a smell I didn't like. There's no such thing as a 'bad' smell for me ... just millions of different odors and combinations, each one unique and intriguing.

"My nose tells me a lot about the people and dogs I meet. It lets me know how they're feeling and where they've been. It tells me where there is something to eat, and it can warn me of danger.

"Naturally, Bill, with your limited ability to smell, you can't do the same. But you can use your other senses to explore and enjoy the present world around you. Take the time to see, smell, hear, taste, touch, and enjoy the people and things you encounter. The world is a wonderful place. Make the effort to appreciate it. You don't need a sensitive snout like mine to do so."

Here he seems to be telling me how to live in the present. Don't just be in the moment, be totally in it and enjoy it to the fullest.

Quotations

"One of the most tragic things I know about human nature is that all of us tend to put off living. We are all dreaming of some magical rose garden over the horizon … instead of enjoying the roses that are blooming outside our windows today."
Dale Carnegie

"Dogs need to sniff the ground; it's how they keep abreast of current events. The ground is a giant dog newspaper, containing all kinds of late-breaking news items, which, if they are especially urgent, are often continued in the next yard."
Dave Barry

"You're only here for a short visit. Don't hurry, don't worry. And be sure to smell the roses along the way."
Walter Hagen

"As you walk down the fairway of life, you must smell the roses, for you only get to play one round."
Ben Hogan

3

Treasure your family

Reilly seems to love everyone. But his relationship with Diane and me is on a whole other level. He always greets us with unrestrained joy. When I asked him why he loves us so much, he cocked his head to the side and thought for a moment before responding.

"Bill, we dogs realize that the foundation of a happy life is our family and our love for them. It began for me at the kennel when I found myself surrounded by five siblings and a loving mom. She fed us whenever we were hungry and taught us some basic rules such as, 'Don't poop where you sleep.' This, by the way, is a good rule for humans as well.

"The seven of us lived together in a 4' by 4' cage. My tummy was always full, my mom was always there, and I could play with my brothers and sisters whenever I wanted. When we got tired, we snuggled up together against our mom's warm body. We didn't have a worry in the world. We were family. We were happy.

"I remember the day when you and Diane came and took me away. I had never been in a car before so the three and a half hour drive was disconcerting to say the least. I didn't know where we were going and I wasn't accustomed to the motion of the car. I had left my brothers and sisters. My mom wasn't around and I didn't know who was going to feed me. That's when I threw up in Diane's lap.

"Then, I thought over the situation. The lap I was sitting on was soft and warm, even if it was then a little damp. The gentle strokes I was getting from Diane were pleasing and comforting. So I asked myself, 'Hey, dummy, what's there not to like?' I was in a different place, but it was a nice place. Besides, there was nothing I could do to change it, so why not accept it?

"At the end of the trip I was taken into your home. It was a giant castle compared to the small cage where I had lived before. You gave me plenty of food. The treats and pats were plentiful. There were good things to chew, and a comfy bed to sleep on. I didn't know what had happened to my old family, but I knew this new one was a keeper.

"I decided I wanted to be with this new family every moment of the day. I vowed to please them and do whatever they wanted … even if it did take a while to figure out what you meant by the weird noises and gestures you directed at me."

It was the same for Diane and myself. Reilly quickly moved from being a new pet to being an integral part of our family … a part that makes it richer, more complete, and, yes, happier.

Quotations

*"The happiest moments of my life have been the few which
I have passed at home in the bosom of my family."*
Thomas Jefferson

*"The bond that links your true family is not one of
blood, but of respect and joy in each other's life."*
Richard Bach

"A family is a place where minds come in contact with one another."
Buddha

"Other things may change us, but we start and end with family"
Anthony Brandt

4

Make friends

"That makes sense to me, Reilly, but you seem to like every person and every dog you meet. How come?"

Reilly gave me a funny look and said, "Bill, I try to make friends with everyone I meet. Why not?

"There's some good in everybody. You just have to find it. It might be as simple as a treat, a gentle pat, or a nice smelling crotch. Learn from us dogs. It's not for nothing that we're called 'man's best friend.'

"But you have to work on a friendship to take it beyond a single interaction to an ongoing relationship. Once you've found a friend, stay close to them. Give them a second, third, or more chances. Enjoy being with them. Be sensitive to their moods and feelings. Be there for them when they need you. Be happy for their joys and sad for their sorrows."

I thought about these wise words and about my own wonderful friends. I concluded that interacting with others expands my life while making friends expands my heart. Reilly has a very big heart.

Quotations

"The one absolutely unselfish friend that man can have in this world, the one that never deserts him, the one that never proves ungrateful or treacherous, is his dog."
George Graham Vest

"One who looks for a friend without faults will have none."
Hasidic Proverb

"The quality of your life is the quality of your relationships."
Anthony Robbins

"Properly trained, a man can be dog's best friend."
Corey Ford

"A friend is a present you give yourself."
Robert Louis Stevenson

"The only way to have a friend is to be one."
Ralph Waldo Emerson

"Friends are the family we choose for ourselves."
Edna Buchanan

5

Kisses are important

"Hey, Reilly, how come you're always licking people, especially me and Diane?"

"Licks are a dog's kisses and they are very important to us, Mr. Bill. What we taste and smell tells us a lot about you. They're also signs of our affection. I could lick you and Diane all day.

"Besides, humans taste good. You've got salt and other stuff on your bodies that are quite yummy. I honestly don't understand why you humans don't kiss each other more. It seems like a great way to get to know new people."

Not everything Reilly says makes human sense. There's no way I'm going to go to a cocktail party and start kissing strangers (even if in some cases I'd like to). However, I can show my interest and affection in other ways.

Quotations

"Happiness is like a kiss … you must share it to enjoy it."
Anonymous

"One kiss breaches the distance between friendship and love."
Anonymous

*"If you make it plain you like people, it's hard
for them to resist liking you back."*
Lois McMaster Bujold

6

Nothing beats face time

"Reilly, you and Gus spend a lot of time together, yet every time you see one another, both of you dogs go nuts. How come?"

"Gus and I are friends. Friends should always be excited to see each other and to be with each other. Humans seem to have lost some of the appreciation of face-to-face contact. You have other means of communication. But these don't come close to the depth and richness of physical contact and proximity when you meet face to face. You're not just exchanging words; you're sharing your entire physical being in a unique, moment in time.

"Gus and I can't talk, write, or use the computer, but even if we could, it could never replace the magic of each time we greet each other. Bill, you should make an effort to see your friends as often as possible and to greet them with enthusiasm and emotion. It will make you feel great and let them know of their importance in your life."

A valid point. Although I am always happy to see my friends, I don't always express that joy clearly. And I don't actively reach out enough to get together with them. Instead, I spend too much time exchanging meaningless emails when I could be having lunch with one of them.

Quotations

*"Without wearing any mask we are conscious of,
we have a special face for each friend."*
Oliver Wendell Holmes

"Better to see the face than to hear the name."
Zen Proverb

*"Electric communication will never be a substitute for the face of someone
who with their soul encourages another person to be brave and true."*
Charles Dickens

7

Love much

"Oh come on, little man," I said with a shrug, "you can't love everybody?"

"Who says?" asked Reilly. "I don't play favorites. I don't see one person or dog as better than another. Sure, they're each different but none of them are 'better.' I love unconditionally in each and every moment. I open my heart to my family, my friends, and all the dogs and people I meet along the way."

He shook his head. "I'm sad when I see dogs that distrust strangers or other dogs. It's not natural. They must have been badly treated as puppies. I feel sorry for them. When dogs are first born, we're little love machines.

"I believe that when you meet someone new, you should assume that he or she is a wonderful person. Often, that will motivate them to be as good as you think they are. If you assume that they're not worth loving, they'll probably live down to your expectations.

"Love makes the world go around. Embrace this concept, Bill, and your world will become a happier, more fulfilling place."

Sometimes it's tough for me to do this. I let petty differences get in the way and sometimes play favorites. Whenever I do, it diminishes me and prevents me from fully appreciating that moment and that person.

Quotations

*"Love life and life will love you back. Love
people and they will love you back."*
Arthur Rubinstein

"A dog is the only thing on earth that loves you more than he loves himself."
Josh Billings

8

Snuggling is sensational

"Reilly, how come you press up against me on the floor and sigh with pleasure whenever I pet you?"

He shook his head and said, "A dog would never ask such a silly question. We are pack animals and snuggling with your pack is a wonderful experience. I clearly remember how warm and wonderful it was to snuggle with my mom and brothers and sisters at the kennel. The warmth from their bodies made me feel peaceful and safe.

"Now, I'm part of your pack, big guy, and I get that same feeling when I lie next to you or Diane. No matter how big or small, all dogs yearn to be lap dogs. If I could fit, and if you'd let me, I'd love to sit on your lap all the time. The next best thing is to lay right by or even on top of your feet."

"I thought it was because my feet smelled."

"There's that too, my friend, that too."

There's no denying the emotional power of touching a loved one. We humans don't do it enough.

Quotations

"At the touch of love, everyone becomes a poet."
Plato

"Without touch we are but hunks of wood."
Jim Morrison

"My little old dog: a heart-beat at my feet."
Edith Wharton

9

To love is to trust

"Reilly, what's that thing all about when you lay on your back and raise your paws in the air? You look like a goof."

"That's my ultimate submission gesture to a human or to another dog. It leaves me completely vulnerable and says, 'I trust you and love you.' Besides, I'm trying to get you to rub my tummy.

"I don't think you humans have anything comparable and if you did, I doubt whether you would ever do it. You don't trust each other enough to make yourself that vulnerable.

"I'm sad for you. By not being able to trust completely, you miss out on a lot … not merely the exquisite pleasure of having your belly rubbed, but also the bond of mutual love and trust that the gesture expresses."

Wow! I never thought about what that strange position meant. It is a pretty clear sign of the unconditional love our four legged friends bless us with.

Quotations

"We're never so vulnerable as when we trust someone."
Walter Anderson

"Few delights can equal the presence of one whom we trust utterly."
George MacDonald

"The best proof of love is trust."
Dr. Joyce Brothers

10

Forgive and forget

"You sound so Pollyanna," I said with a shake of my head. "Surely you don't love someone after they've hurt or been mean to you?"

"I don't like it when people or dogs do stuff like that. But I learned back in the kennel that it was better to forgive one of my brothers when he hurt me than it was to inflate my ego and hold a grudge.

"Harboring real or imagined slights is destructive and unproductive. What difference does it make in the long run?

"I believe most dogs are like me. I don't care that you accidentally stepped on me or kept me locked up all day. No one has ever had to tell me to, 'Get over it!' As soon as it's over, it's over, and I'll love you just as before."

I was beginning to look at Reilly in a totally different light. He wasn't so happy because of some genetic predisposition as I had first assumed. His life was an on-going series of conscious decisions to be happy in each present moment. I resolved to try to do the same.

Quotations

"Holding on to anger, resentment, and hurt only gives you tense muscles, a headache, and a sore jaw from clenching your teeth. Forgiveness gives you back laughter and the lightness in your life."
Joan Lunden
Healthy Living Magazine

"Friendship flourishes at the fountain of forgiveness."
William Arthur Ward

"Forgiveness means letting go of the past."
Gerald Jampolsky

"Forgive, forget. Bear with the faults of others, as you would have them bear with yours. Be patient and understanding. Life is too short to be vengeful or malicious."
Phillip Brooks

"While seeking revenge, dig two graves ... one for yourself."
Doug Horton

"To forgive is to set a prisoner free and discover that the prisoner was you."
Lewis B. Smedes

11

Anger is a waste of time

"Okay, Reilly, you can forgive others, but don't you ever get angry? What if one of your brothers back in the kennel ate your dinner or bit too hard? Didn't that tick you off?"

Reilly shrugged. "Maybe for a nanosecond. But once the moment was over, I would have put it aside and enjoyed the next moment rather than trying to relive the past.

"I have met some dogs that must have been mistreated. They snarl or bark out their anger trying to prove their toughness or superiority. I am genuinely puzzled when I see dogs do this. What a waste of the present moment. It's just so ... so human.

"I only bark when I want to play with another dog or when I sense a potential threat to our home. As you know, a stranger coming to our window will get such a greeting from me. But, as you also know, once you have greeted him and let him into our castle, my growl will be replaced by a smile and a sniff of his crotch."

I think this would be a pretty good policy for humans, too ... except maybe for the crotch sniff.

Quotations

"Revenge is often like biting a dog because the dog bit you."
Austin O'Malley

*"Speak when you are angry … and you will make
the best speech you'll ever regret."*
Lawrence J. Peter

*"What I've learned about being angry with people is that
it generally hurts you more than it hurts them."*
Oprah Winfrey

"Anger is never without a reason, but seldom with a good one."
Benjamin Franklin

*"You will not be punished for your anger, you
will be punished by your anger."*
Buddha

*"Holding on to anger is like grasping a hot coal with the intent of
throwing it at someone else; you are the one who gets burned."*
Buddha

12

Be curious and direct

"You're an awfully curious creature, Reilly. You always have to find out what Diane or I are doing. You want to see what it is, smell what it's about, and even lick it if you can. How come?"

"As I've said before, Mr. Bill, we dogs experience the present through all our senses. When I see you guys doing something new, I gotta check it out. You're my pack and I want to see everything my pack is up to. And, as you implied, I'm not shy about it. I just go up to you and stick my snout in.

"In my humble, canine opinion, most humans would be a lot better off if they were more direct instead of tip-toeing around and peeking over their shoulders. They're afraid of looking foolish by being direct about their curiosity. But, curiosity is a wonderful impulse. It teaches us new things. Dogs know this and don't mind looking foolish … in fact, it's kind of fun."

I got his point. Curiosity leads to more knowledge and new experiences. Unfortunately, it's hard for me to overcome the social norms about minding my own business. It's even harder to let myself look foolish.

Quotations

"I think, at a child's birth, if a mother could ask a fairy godmother to endow it with the most useful gift, that gift would be curiosity."
Eleanor Roosevelt

"Satisfaction of one's curiosity is one of the greatest sources of happiness in life."
Dr. Linus Pauling

"Curiosity killed the cat, but where human beings are concerned, the only thing a healthy curiosity can kill is ignorance."
Harry Lorayne

"The greatest pleasure of a dog is that you may make a fool of yourself with him, and not only will he not scold you, but he will make a fool of himself too."
Samuel Butler

13

Don't sweat the big stuff

Reilly sat up. "Unlike you human folks, I don't worry about the meaning of life, retirement funds, the cost of health care, or the political situation. I am delighted to let you lose sleep and get indigestion over such matters.

"My world is a simple one where joy lies in small things; the arrival of a visitor, the smells on a walk, or the neat stick I just found. If you're honest with yourself, you'll realize that most of the big stuff in life is out of your control. Worrying about it only robs you of the real joy of the moment."

"Easy for you to say, my furry freeloader, but if we both want to eat, I've got to worry about some of that stuff."

"Excellent point, my most generous, handsome, and intelligent master. Believe me when I say I really appreciate that and don't envy your responsibility. I just wish you'd keep that stuff in proper perspective. There's a big difference between thinking about something and worrying about something. Thinking can be very constructive; worrying can be very destructive."

The little man sure knows how to suck up to me, doesn't he? But once again, his point is valid. It's okay to plan to make something happen, but just worrying will never make anything happen and will ruin the present.

Quotations

*"If you can solve your problem, then what is the need of worrying?
If you cannot solve it, then what is the use of worrying?"*
Shantideva

*"There is a great difference between worry and concern. A worried
person sees a problem, and a concerned person solves a problem."*
Harold Stephens

"Worry never robs tomorrow of its sorrow, it only saps today of its joy."
Leo F. Buscaglia

*"Don't accept your dog's admiration as conclusive
evidence that you are wonderful."*
Ann Landers

14

Don't give in to fear

"Reilly, you seem to be fearless. I don't think I've ever seen you scared."

"Hey, big guy, I can be startled as much as the next dog. However, there's a big difference between scared and startled. If you drop a kitchen pot on the floor beside me, I'm gonna react big time. I'd have to be both deaf and dumb not to.

"But then, I'll check it out and see that the noise came from one of those big things you put on the stove. I'll see that there's no threat to me. Maybe I'll sniff it just to be sure. Then, I'll move on.

"Being scared is different. That is caused either by a perceived threat or an irrational fear that you humans often seem to have. Fortunately for me, you and Diane make my world a very safe place so there are no actual threats. I'm a dog and by definition not rational, so I don't have irrational fears.

"Examine your fears, Bill. I think you'll find most of them are irrational. Get rid of them. They are projections of the still nonexistent future that rob you of happiness in the present."

Of course, he's right again. Most fear, like worry, comes from not living in the present and from imagining what might happen in a hypothetical future.

Quotations

"There is no terror in a bang, only in the anticipation of it."
Alfred Hitchcock

*"Most fears cannot withstand the test of careful scrutiny
and analysis. When we expose our fears to the light of
thoughtful examination, they usually just evaporate."*
Jack Canfield

*"You can conquer almost any fear if you will only make up your mind to
do so. For remember, fear doesn't exist anywhere except in the mind."*
Dale Carnegie

15

If it feels good, do it

Reilly stretched. "Another thing that prevents you humans from enjoying the present are all the 'shoulda', 'woulda', 'coulda's' that mess up your brains. You'll never catch me wondering whether or not I 'should' do something. I just do it. If it feels good, I'll do it again. Why not? Don't over think things. Don't postpone things 'for a better time.' The present is the only time you'll ever have.

"Don't let your 'shoulds' block you from happiness. It seems to me that a lot of humans get so caught up in analyzing whether or not they should do something, they miss out on the enjoyment of the present and on much of the fun that life can offer. It's your life and your moment. Go for it!"

I should do this.

Quotations

"Enjoy yourself … it's later than you think."
Socrates

"A man should look for what is, and not for what he thinks it should be."
Albert Einstein

"My dog is usually pleased with what I do, because she is not infected with the concept of what I 'should' be doing."
Lonzo Idolswine

16

Be passionate

"But it's more than just doing it, Reilly. You always go from moment to moment and action to action with intensity and enthusiasm. How do you do that?"

"Easy, big man, because I only do what turns me on … what I'm passionate about. I realize that's easy for me to say since I don't have to do all of those housekeeping, planning, and administrative tasks that you do. I don't know how anyone could be passionate about that stuff.

"But be passionate about the stuff that you choose to do in your free time. You seem to do some things, Bill, just because you can or because they're what you usually do. However, you often don't seem to enjoy doing them. You just go through the motions of completing them.

"I only choose stuff that turns me on, stuff I can completely throw myself into. When you choose such stuff, it's easy to be enthusiastic. Be passionate about the stuff you do. Your life will be richer and fuller for it."

He's right about that. Too often I do things such as read a magazine or watch television just because that's what I usually do at that time. I don't stop to ask myself, "What do I really want to do now? What will excite me now?"

Quotations

"I had learnt to seek intensity ... more of life, a concentrated sense of life."
Nina Berberova

"Passion is energy. Feel the power that comes
from focusing on what excites you."
Oprah Winfrey

"Love life, engage in it, give it all you've got. Love it with a passion,
because life truly does give back, many times over, what you put into it."
Maya Angelou

17

Be spontaneous

Reilly shook his head and looked at me with a sad expression. "You humans really make it hard on yourselves. You try to prepare for all possible situations and plan out everything in advance. For you to do anything requires this enormous effort. However, as you're doing all this, there are precious, one of a kind moments zooming by. These are moments never to be experienced again.

"Dogs ignore all that preparation stuff and just do it. We are constantly spontaneous in the present moment. I'm sorry to say, Bill, that I don't think I've ever seen you doing anything completely spontaneous.

"I realize it's difficult for you, my friend. But you owe it to yourself to try. Be spontaneous! Start with something little like raising your head to the rain or giving a friend a hug for no reason. You'll be amazed at how pleasurable it is! By side stepping that mental control system, you get to enjoy the present in a totally different and more powerful way."

Of course, he's right again. I've started to do some little things just because I want to and it feels wonderful and right.

Quotations

"Spontaneity is the quality of being able to do something just because you feel like it at the moment, of trusting your instincts, of taking yourself by surprise, and snatching from the clutches of your well-organized routine, a bit of unscheduled play."
Unknown

"Our spontaneous action is always the best. You cannot, with your best deliberation and heed, come so close to any question as your spontaneous glance shall bring you."
Ralph Waldo Emerson

"Analysis kills spontaneity. The grain once ground into flour springs and germinates no more."
Henri Frederic Amiel

18

Live in hope

"Okay, my wise little man," I said, "if you're always so into the present, how can you make the future better? Is 'now' all there is?"

"It's not the future that can get better, Bill. The future hasn't happened yet. Only the present can be 'better'. Dogs realize this and constantly hope that the present moment will be better. Hope is like a religion to us. We believe that every moment will bring us something good, something wonderful … *in that moment.*

"When you go near the fridge, I assume you're getting something for me. When you go near the door, I think we must be going for a walk. When I see a new person or dog, I'm sure they'll want to be my best friend. Hope is a wonderful now to live in."

I thought of how I have changed over the years, how some of the hope I had as a young man has been slowly eroded by doubt and cynicism. I vowed to overcome that erosion. Reilly is right. Hope is a great place to be.

Quotations

*"Hope is important because it can make the
present moment less difficult to bear."*
Thich Nhat Hanh

"Hope is only the love of life."
Henri-Frederic Amiel

"Hope arouses, as nothing else can arouse, a passion for the possible."
William Sloan Coffin

19

Have realistic expectations

"If you live in hope all the time, Reilly, you must be constantly disappointed when what you hope for doesn't happen."

"You don't get it, my friend. I hope in the present moment, and then I hope in the next moment. I don't stop and say, 'Gosh, I didn't get what I hoped for in that last moment.' You humans do that a lot and it's a colossal waste of time and energy.

"Besides, I keep my expectations minimal and basic. I don't hope to win the lottery or have dinner in Paris. I just want to be with you and Diane. If I happen to get a treat in that moment, that's icing on the cake. If I don't get a treat, that's wonderful, too. If your expectations are low and centered on the present, you'll never be disappointed."

By any kind of measurement I've led and still lead a wonderful life. Yet, I frequently ruin my present moment when I feel disappointed that my life isn't 'better'.

Quotations

"Expect nothing. Live frugally on surprise."
Alice Walker

"The best things in life are unexpected – because there were no expectations."
Eli Khamarov

"Disappointment is a sort of bankruptcy... the bankruptcy of a soul that expends too much in hope and expectation."
Eric Hoffer

"It is generally known that he who expects much will be often disappointed."
Samuel Johnson

"Happiness equals reality minus expectations."
Tom Magliozzi

"When one's expectations are reduced to zero, one really appreciates everything one does have."
Stephen Hawking

20

Keep learning

Reilly closed his eyes in thought. "Remember when I said how wonderful it was when I first got to your house? The only bad part about it was that I couldn't understand what you wanted me to do. You kept making all these strange noises and hand gestures. It was so weird because I didn't have a clue what they meant.

"You see, we dogs want to please. Doing what you would like us to do makes us happy. You just have to be patient and take the time to teach us what it is you want.

"I'm a dog and I love to learn new things. I feel good when I do. The praise, hugs, and treats I get for learning are added bonuses. The saying, 'You can't teach an old dog new tricks,' is rubbish. It is spouted by lazy old masters that choose to not teach their dogs new stuff. I love to learn, but please teach me with the same energy and enthusiasm as you did when I was a puppy."

Isn't it the same for us humans? The people who continue to learn and continue to challenge themselves as they grow older are the healthiest and the happiest.

Quotations

"Live as if you were to die tomorrow. Learn as if you will live forever."
Mahatma Gandhi

"Always keep learning. It keeps you young."
Patty Berg

"What is important is to keep learning, to enjoy challenge, and to tolerate ambiguity. In the end there are no certain answers."
Martina Horner

"The old saw about old dogs and new tricks only applies to certain people."
Daniel Pinkwater

21

Pay attention

"Reilly, how did you know I was sad the other day? You came over to me, laid your head on my lap, and gave me a look that clearly said, 'It's okay, big guy. Everything will be all right.'"

"I'm a mind reader," he replied with a smile. "Just kidding, boss man. Contrary to some people's opinion, dogs are not psychic. If we seem to be at times, it's simply because we pay more attention to our masters and the world around us than you humans do. We look ... really look at your face. We watch your movements and gestures. We listen to the tone of your voice. We can actually smell some of your emotions. All this usually gives us a clear picture of your state of mind.

"People can't smell like dogs can. But you can look and listen. Unfortunately, most humans don't seem to take the time and effort to really observe and listen to one another in the present moment. You're too distracted, too worried about other stuff. You think of other things, regret the past, or worry about the future. If you really did pay close attention in the present moment, you could be a mind reader too."

I still think the little guy is psychic. He seems to know things about me that I don't know myself.

Quotations

"Give whatever you are doing and whomever you are with the gift of your attention."
Jim Rohn

"Silence may be golden, but can you think of a better way to entertain someone than to listen to him?"
Brigham Young

"It's funny how dogs and cats know the inside of folks better than other folks do, isn't it?"
Eleanor H. Parker

"One reason a dog can be such a comfort when you're feeling blue is that he doesn't try to find out why."
Unknown

22

Be your own dog

"We dogs are pack animals, Bill. We love to get together to play. I think that's what I miss most about leaving my original family. I always had a great time with my brothers and sisters.

"But being in a pack doesn't mean surrendering your own character and identity. There were many times when I thought my siblings were acting like idiots and I wanted no part of it. Remember when you first came to see me and my brothers and sisters behaved like twits? They barked and yelped and tossed themselves against the gate like moths against a light bulb.

"Not me. I just observed their nonsense and checked you and Diane out. Who were you? Why were you looking at my family? Why were you pointing at me and talking to Arlene, the boss of the kennel?

"Being your own dog, or man in your case, is more than just standing apart from the pack. It's thinking for yourself. It's having your own core principles and beliefs. Since I don't do much heavy thinking, mine are pretty simple and revolve around making myself happy.

"No matter how complex and detailed your human principles and beliefs are, big guy, they should revolve around the same thing ... making yourself happy."

The breeder didn't call him a "monk" and "thinker" for nothing. Once again he proved his happiness was based not just on luck or a genetic predisposition. It is a conscious choice about how he lives his life.

Quotations

"Think for yourselves and let others enjoy the privilege to do so, too."
Voltaire

"Think wrongly, if you please, but in all cases think for yourself."
Doris Lessing

"A man who does not think for himself does not think at all."
Oscar Wilde

"Independence – is loyalty to one's best self and principles, and this is often disloyalty to the general idols and fetishes."
Mark Twain

"Independence is happiness."
Susan B. Anthony

"It is not easy to find happiness in ourselves, and it is not possible to find it elsewhere."
Agnes Repplier

"Live your own life, for you will die your own death."
Latin Proverb

23

Ignore what others think

"Hey, Reilly, are you ever bothered by what other dogs think about you?" He made a noise deep in his throat that sounded an awful lot like a snort.

"I don't know how to break this to you, big guy, but we dogs don't 'think about each other like you humans do about one another. A dog is a dog. When I think about my buddy, Gus, I don't make any judgments about him. I don't rank him versus other dogs as to how smart or how attractive he is. He's just Gus and I'm just Reilly. All I think about is how he smells and how much fun we have playing together. That's all that's important to me.

"Humans, on the other hand, seem to try and rank one another on every possible attribute and ability. 'John is good at this.' 'Alice talks too much.' 'George is overweight.' It's a vicious circle because you know they're doing the same thing to you. Therefore, you start worrying about where they're putting you in their own rankings. What a silly exercise in ego justification and what a colossal waste of time!

"Stop judging others and ignore what judgments others may make of you. If you like playing with John, Alice, or George, go ahead and play. That's all that's important."

He made a very good point but one that's tough to put in practice. I'm trying hard not to judge and not to care about what others think of me. It doesn't always work, but just being aware of the fact that I'm doing it, helps me overcome it.

Quotations

*"A wise man makes his own decisions, an
ignorant man follows public opinion."*
Chinese Proverb

*"If you want to reach a state of bliss, then go beyond your ego and
the internal dialogue. Make a decision to relinquish the need to
control, the need to be approved, and the need to judge."*
Deepak Chopra

*"One should respect public opinion insofar as is necessary to avoid
starvation and keep out of prison, but anything that goes beyond
this is voluntary submission to an unnecessary tyranny."*
Bertrand Russell

24

Lighten up

"Bill, I hope you don't take this the wrong way, but sometimes you get all riled up about the silliest things. If someone doesn't return your call, or you do something that doesn't work out very well, you tend to act like it's the end of the world.

"You'll never catch me doing that. If Gus doesn't want to play with me, that's fine. Gus can do whatever he wants. If something I do isn't perfect, so what? It's done and now is an entirely new and different moment.

So lighten up, my friend. Life is short. Don't ruin the present by taking yourself so seriously.

He's right again, and don't we all do it? When I think back at events and situations that have upset me, they are usually incredibly trivial. I take them as "important" because I've projected some imaginary ego importance upon them. I have to realize the insignificance of such things.

Quotations

"Drop the idea that you are Atlas carrying the world on your shoulders. The world would go on even without you. Don't take yourself so seriously."
Norman Vincent Peale

"Take everything you like seriously, except yourselves."
Rudyard Kipling

"It is a curious fact that people are never so trivial as when they take themselves seriously."
Oscar Wilde

"Do not take life too seriously; you will never get out of it alive."
Elbert Hubbard

25

Smile often

Reilly looked up at me with his mouth open and his tongue hanging out.

"Why are you smiling, Reilly?" I asked.

"Because I'm happy to be with you, my friend. For dogs, smiling is an expression of our happiness. When we are enjoying ourselves, we smile. Some humans think we smile when we open our mouths and pant. Others think we smile when we wag our tails. They're both right.

"However, when we're really, really happy, we smile with our whole body. Look at me closely when I'm very happy. My tail wags wildly, my butt goes from side to side, I open my mouth, my tongue hangs out, I breathe quickly, and I prance about.

"You have to admit, my friend, that whenever I do those things, you feel happier yourself. Smiling is contagious. It infects everyone around you. You should try to express your happiness with not just a smile but with your whole being. It will make you feel even better and make those around you happier as well."

I can still picture him saying this and prancing about with a huge smile. The proof of his words was in the pudding. I couldn't stop myself from smiling back at him.

Quotations

"Smile, it is the key that fits the lock of everyone's heart."
Anthony J. D'Angelo

*"Every time you smile at someone, it is an action of
love, a gift to that person, a beautiful thing."*
Saint Teresa of Calcutta

*"Man himself cannot express love and humility by external signs
so plainly as does a dog, when with drooping ears, hanging lips,
flexuous body, and wagging tail, he meets his beloved master."*
Charles Darwin

"A dog wags its tail with its heart."
Martin Buxbaum

26

Run with the wind

Reilly got up and stretched. "I love my body. It lets me smell, taste, see, feel, and move. It's magical!

"There is nothing more exhilarating than running full out on a bright summer day or a snow covered winter afternoon. I love feeling the power of my muscles pulling me along. I love the rush of the wind on my face.

"I put that same total commitment into every moment and everything I do, even when I'm just eating or sleeping. It makes me feel alive!

"You humans often seem to only commit halfway to things and appear embarrassed to let your emotions show. Don't be a couch potato. Be a dog! Put your whole self into it. Do lots of physical stuff and enjoy being alive."

I've started trying to do this every day; to commit fully to things, to be more physical, to be more active. I feel better when I do and enjoy whatever I'm doing more.

Quotations

"Try to learn to breathe deeply, really to taste food when you eat, and when you sleep, really sleep. Try as much as possible to be wholly alive with all your might, and when you laugh, laugh like hell …Try to be alive. You will be dead soon enough."
William Saroyan

"The difference between involvement and commitment is like ham and eggs. The chicken is involved; the pig is committed."
Martina Navratilova

"Commitment unlocks the doors of imagination, allows vision, and gives us the 'right stuff' to turn our dreams into reality."
James Womack

27

Doing nothing is something

"As I've told you, Bill, dogs love physical activity. But the opposite is also true. We love to relax, to lie down … to do absolutely nothing. We love to just be.

"You humans, on the other hand, seem to think there is something wrong with doing nothing. You rush around all day. You listen to music while you walk and drive. You always need something to do and treat 'relaxation' as if it's a dirty word. If someone comes in while you're looking out the window and asks you what you're doing, you get embarrassed and make up something out of guilt to hide your imagined laziness. Don't deny it, my friend. I've heard you do it.

"Dogs know that doing nothing is not only acceptable, it's important. It recharges the batteries and lets you better appreciate the beauty of now. You should do nothing more often."

I thought about what Reilly had said and realized how true it was. I always have to be doing something, whether I'm sitting in the backyard or waiting in line. I bring a book with me to an appointment … just in case I have to wait and there is, God forbid, nothing to do. I vowed to start doing some nothing everyday.

Quotations

"Time you enjoyed wasting is not wasted."
John Lennon

*"Your mind will answer most questions if you
learn to relax and wait for the answer."*
William S. Burroughs

*"Happiness is a butterfly, which when pursued, is always just beyond your
grasp, but which, if you will sit down quietly, may alight upon you."*
Nathaniel Hawthorne

*"To sit with a dog on a hillside on a glorious afternoon is to be back
in Eden, where doing nothing was not boring – it was peace."*
Milan Kundera

28

Walks are wonderful

"Tell me something else, Reilly. Why do you always get so excited when I ask you if you want to go outside for a walk?"

He tilted his head to the side and stared at me with an expression that indicated he thought this was the stupidest question he had ever heard. "Think about it, big guy. You can go out anytime you like. You can go anywhere you want. You can stay out as long as you want. I, on the other hand, am confined to the castle. Don't get me wrong; it's a wonderful castle full of good stuff and my favorite people. I love it here, but I also like to experience other things.

"In addition to the physical activity, walks let me explore the world. I get to see new things and smell new scents. I meet other dogs and get to smell their butts. I also meet new people and get to smell their crotches. You can't even imagine how much fun that is if you have a nose like mine!

"I've never gone on a walk I didn't like. I view my leash as a means of liberation, not as a constraint. Whatever the weather, walks are the best parts of the day. I know you walk with me a lot and I'm always happy to have you by my side. However, you should go on some walks by yourself, my friend, and smell those roses."

This is another valid point from my furry philosopher. I enjoy and get a lot out of my walks with him. However, walking by myself lets me think more clearly and enjoy the moment solely on my terms.

Quotations

"If it wasn't for dogs, some people would never go for a walk."
Unknown

"Few people know how to take a walk. The qualifications are endurance, plain clothes, old shoes, an eye for nature, good humor, vast curiosity, good speech, good silence, and nothing too much."
Ralph Waldo Emerson

"That's the best thing about walking, the journey itself. It doesn't matter much whether you get where you're going or not. You'll get there anyway."
Edward Abbey

"In every walk with nature one receives far more than he seeks."
John Muir

"In my walks I would fain return to my senses."
Henry David Thoreau

"And remember, no matter where you go, there you are."
Confucius

29

Window on the world

"Another question, little man," I asked. "Why do you spend so much time looking out the window?"

"Because that's where the world is, my friend. Since I can't let myself out to go for a walk, I sit and look out the window for hours at a time with only the occasional break for a nice snooze. It's even better when the window is open and I can use this super snout. Looking out at the world is a lot better than looking at that stupid electronic box that you stare at each night for hours.

"I enjoy every person or animal that walks by, every bird that flies, and every leaf that blows. It's not as good as going for a walk, but it is real … it's now. Take the time to look out your window, Bill. Enjoy the view. Enjoy your now."

I realized that this applied to many things in life. Every moment brings a new window to experience and enjoy.

Quotations

"Birth is the sudden opening of a window, through which you look out upon a stupendous prospect."
William MacNeile Dixon

"Our senses are indeed our doors and windows on this world, in a very real sense the key to the unlocking of meaning and the wellspring of creativity."
Jean Houston

"Did you ever notice when you blow in a dog's face, he gets mad at you? But when you take him in a car, he sticks his head out the window."
Steve Bluestone

30

Sit and think

"Okay, little man, I get the window thing, but sometimes I see you just sitting and staring at nothing in particular. What's up with that?"

"Guilty as charged, my friend. When I'm not looking at the world going by and not quite ready for a nap, I like to think about stuff. It's not heavy stuff like you humans do. And it's not about the past or the future. It's more an enjoyment of the moment. I think about the things that are really important to me such as; how my body feels, how pleasant my surroundings are, how lucky I am to have you and Diane, and how much fun it is to play with Cosmo.

"You should do the same, Bill. Whenever you have a free moment, meditate on the happiness of the moment, the things that are really important to you, and the joy of being alive."

He's right, of course. I realized how little time I take each day, if any, to appreciate the truly important things in my life and how much time I waste doing busy work or fretting about the inconsequential.

Quotations

"Remember happiness doesn't depend upon who you are or what you have; it depends solely on what you think."
Dale Carnnegie

"We must always think about things, and we must think about things as they are, not as they are said to be."
George Bernard Shaw

"The more man meditates upon good thoughts, the better will be his world and the world at large."
Confucius

"Those who know how to think need no teachers."
Mahatma Gandhi

"What we think, we become."
Buddha

31

A stick is just a stick

"Reilly, sometimes when we're walking, you'll pick up a tiny piece of branch and proudly hold it in your mouth. Then, you'll drop it for no apparent reason. The next moment, you'll pick up a limb twice as long as you are and carry it around like it's the Holy Grail. What's that all about?"

"Bill, you humans are obsessed with material possessions. You need to possess all this stuff to prove your self worth, yet most of it just sits there gathering dust. Why have it at all?

"Dogs don't need much stuff besides food and love. Mind you, a good chew toy and a comfy place to sleep are also nice.

"That doesn't mean I don't appreciate some stuff. When I go outside for instance, I love to find a good stick; short or long, thick or thin … they are all great fun to me. I can carry them as a trophy or chew them like a toy. However, when all is said and done, a stick is just a stick. I can drop it whenever and wherever I want and never look back cause it's just stuff … stuff that I decided to have fun with, but stuff that I don't need and can walk away from.

"You should do the same with all of your stuff. Have fun with it but don't ever forget that it's just stuff. There are a lot more important and enjoyable things in life."

After he said this, I walked through our house and took notice of all my "stuff." How right Reilly was! The vast majority of all my possessions are just stuff that I really don't need.

Quotations

"A dog owns nothing, yet is seldom dissatisfied."
Irish Proverb

*"No matter how little money and how few possessions
you own, having a dog makes you rich."*
Louis Sabin

"Treasure your relationships, not your possessions."
Anthony J. D'Angelo

*"Happiness resides not in possessions, and not in
gold, happiness dwells in the soul."*
Democritus

*"My most treasured possessions are not things, they are only
things. My friends, family, and animals are what counts."*
Olivia Newton-John

32

Guilt is a waste of time

Reilly got up for a drink of water then sat down again and said, "All this yapping is making me thirsty. I don't know how you humans do it all day. By the way, one thing that I forgot to mention earlier is that humans are hung up on guilt, whether it's guilt about things that you've done, guilt about things you should have done, or guilt about things you want to do. It's just so unproductive. All living creatures make decisions everyday about what they do and when they do it. It's just the natural order of things. If we didn't make such decisions, we would never do anything.

"I make my decisions based on what will please me the most. Sometimes it is running around like crazy. Sometimes it's licking myself. Sometimes it's making you happy because making you happy makes me happy. Unfortunately, sometimes my choices make you unhappy. It's not that I want to make you unhappy, I'm just trying to make myself happy. It's that simple, and I don't feel at all guilty about it.

"Feeling guilt is like living your life in hindsight. We dogs are fortunate; we don't have hindsight … or foresight for that matter. The only hindsight we have is when we look at another dog's rear end. For me that's' a heck of lot more pleasurable than feeling useless guilt about some decision that I made in the past.

"So don't be so hard on yourself, big guy. From what I can tell, you always try to do the right thing and to make the best decision. That's all anyone or any dog can do. Accept the fact that you'll be wrong occasionally. When you are, learn from it and move on."

I was so busy thinking about things I felt guilty about at the time that it was only much later that I realized Reilly had given me a big compliment. I felt guilty about not thanking him.

Quotations

"Look through the window, not the rearview mirror."
Byrd Baggett

"Guilt: the gift that keeps on giving."
Erma Bombeck

"Guilt is anger directed at ourselves."
Peter McWilliams

"Nagging guilt is like gray paint splashed over life's sparkling moments."
Sally Shannon

33

Being first isn't important

Reilly stood up and did one of those whole body shakes that dogs love to do. "Bill, remember that old slogan, 'If you're not the lead dog the view is always the same?' A lot of humans seem to think that means you've got to be number one or you're a loser.

"That's rubbish. If all dogs and all humans were to follow that principle, we would be constantly fighting each other trying to prove we're the best. Besides, as I've already mentioned, the view of a follower is a very enjoyable one from a dog's perspective.

Being number one is vastly overrated. Mind you, there's nothing wrong with it, it's just that it's not worth making yourself miserable trying to get there and then killing yourself trying to stay there.

"Too many people spend their lives being so competitive that they never appreciate their present moment and the view they have in that moment. Life is too short. Don't do things just to be better than someone else. Do stuff that makes you better, that makes you happier. Enjoy whatever view you have and be happy to be alive."

He makes another good point. Too often I have stressed myself out trying to show how good or smart I am. For what purpose? I am who I am and all the effort in the world isn't going to change that.

Quotations

"Winning is important to me, but what brings me real joy is the experience of being fully engaged in whatever I'm doing."
Phil Jackson

"Don't bother just to be better than your contemporaries or predecessors. Try to be better than yourself."
William Faulkner

"The only competition worthy a wise man is with himself."
Anna Jameson

"Enjoy the journey, enjoy every moment, and quit worrying about winning and losing."
Matt Biondi

"The problem with winning the rat race is you're still a rat."
Lily Tomlin

34

Keep your sense of wonder

Reilly looked around. "You know, Bill, this is a beautiful world we live in. It's full of good things and delightful surprises. As a dog, I'm frequently surprised, probably because I don't have that human foresight/planning stuff getting in the way.

"As a result of this, I'm constantly in a state of wonder. Each moment brings another exciting surprise. Pardon the pun, but they're wonder 'full' surprises.

"You humans are born with the same sense of wonder. However, it seems to me that as you get older you start to lose it and don't appreciate the surprises you encounter as much as you once did. That's why dogs love kids. They're still like us; they're full of wonder.

"Don't ever lose your sense of wonder, Bill. Cherish that childlike awe of the universe around you, of the people, places, and events in your life."

Once again, my little furry professor had given me something important to think about. How sad it is that so many of us equate "maturity" with a bland, non-emotional acceptance of reality.

Quotations

"He who can no longer pause to wonder and stand rapt
in awe, is as good as dead; his eyes are closed."
Albert Einstein

"The possession of knowledge does not kill the sense of
wonder and mystery. There is always more mystery."
Anais Nin

"To be surprised, to wonder, is to begin to understand."
Jose Ortega y Gasset

"Never say there is nothing beautiful in the world anymore. There is always
something to make you wonder in the shape of a tree, the trembling of a leaf."
Albert Schweitzer

"Whether sixty or sixteen, there is in every human being's
heart the lure of wonder, the unfailing child-like appetite
of what's next, and the joy of the game of living."
Samuel Ullman

35

Sleep is a good thing

Reilly yawned, laid down, and almost immediately fell asleep. It didn't bother me. It was a warm summer's day and I had a lot of his canine counsel to ponder ... part of which was just being there and enjoying the moment. A half hour later, he awoke and went through his usual routine of three or four immense yawns and several full body stretches.

"I have to say, Reilly, that you really seem to love sleeping and can do so at the drop of a hat. Why do you sleep so much?"

He lowered his head in thought and then looked up. "Because I want to. You humans seem to think sleep is just a necessary evil that stops you from doing important stuff. Not me. Sleep to me is an art form, a deliciously pleasant activity.

"I don't worry about what else I should be doing. Sleep is important physically and emotionally. I sleep a lot and when I wake up I'm refreshed and ready for anything."

Here was one place where I am totally on Reilly's philosophical wavelength. I, too, love to sleep and don't feel at all guilty about it.

Quotations

"Sleep is the best meditation."
Dalai Lama

"Sleep is the golden chain that ties health and our bodies together."
Thomas Dekker

"It is a common experience that a problem difficult at night is resolved in the morning after the committee of sleep has worked on it."
John Steinbeck

"There is only one thing people like that is good for them; a good night's sleep."
Edgar Watson Howe

36

You don't have to understand

Reilly sat up to make a point. "Bill, when you ask me all these questions it reminds me of how obsessed humans are about trying to understand everything.

"Not us dogs. In a sense you could say that the principle of 'ignorance is bliss,' is another component of canine happiness that you should embrace. For example, I don't know where my food comes from. I don't understand how it's made. I don't know how it's paid for. And you know what? I don't care. All I know is it tastes good and fills my tummy.

"You humans always want to understand everything completely. You think that such understanding will give you power over the world around you. You get nervous when you don't understand why something is happening or not happening. The result is that many times you fail to enjoy the taste and fullness of life. Learn to enjoy the experience with or without the explanation."

Another simple point so obvious that the little guy once again made me feel stupid.

Quotations

"A man's ignorance sometimes is not only useful, but beautiful – while his knowledge, so called, is often times worse than useless, besides being ugly."
Henry David Thoreau,
Excursions

"Sometimes it proves the highest understanding not to understand."
Baltasar Gracian

"The greatest wisdom often consists in ignorance."
Baltasar Gracian

"Everybody experiences far more than he understands. Yet it is experience, rather than understanding that influences behavior."
Marshall McLuhan

"The true sign of intelligence is not knowledge but imagination."
Albert Einstein

"To know is to know that you know nothing. That is the meaning of true knowledge."
Confucius

37

Accept what is

"Reilly, except for the times when you're playing with Gus, Cosmo, or another dog, you're always so calm. You look like there is nowhere else you'd rather be, nothing else you'd rather be doing. How come?"

"And why shouldn't I, Mr. Bill? It's just another way of living in the present. Whether I'm wrestling with a friend, looking out the window, or watching you and Diane eating, that's my reality. That's my present moment. That's what is.

Thinking about doing something else or being some other place is just a futile avoidance of that reality. I know you humans do that a lot. Whenever you do, you rob yourselves of the happiness of the present moment. Happiness comes from accepting what is. There is no other reality."

Can't argue with his logic. Unfortunately, I find myself too often not following this wise advice.

Quotations

"If I could define enlightenment briefly, I would say it is 'the quiet acceptance of what is.'"
Wayne Dyer

"The greatest gift that you can give to others is the gift of unconditional love and acceptance."
Brian Tracy

"Happiness can exist only in acceptance."
George Orwell

38

Be patient

"I'm always amazed by your patience, little man. You always know when it's time for dinner and, in case we forget, you remind us with a look or a gentle nudge. If we're busy doing something or talking to someone and don't get around to feeding you for a half hour or more later than usual, you don't get upset. You just lie down and wait. You're an awfully patient fellow."

"Thank you, my friend, but why shouldn't I be? It's part of accepting what is. If you guys don't want to feed me for some reason, my getting upset isn't going to get rid of my hunger. So, I'll just let you know it's that time and then wait for that food moment to arrive."

He's right again. Impatience accomplishes nothing. It just upsets us and robs us of our enjoyment of the present moment.

Quotations

"Patience is the companion of wisdom."
Saint Augustine

"He that can have Patience can have what he will."
Benjamin Franklin

"The key to everything is patience. You get the chicken by hatching the egg, not by smashing it."
Arnold H. Glasgow

"Our patience will achieve more than our force."
Edmund Burke

"It is not necessary for all men to be great in action. The greatest and sublimest power is often simple patience."
Horace Bushnell

39

Never give up

"When you set your mind on something, Reilly, such as chasing a squirrel or eating a marrow bone, it's almost impossible to get you to stop. Is that because you're stubborn?"

"That may be part of it, Bill, but you make it sound like stubbornness is a bad thing. I see nothing wrong in setting a goal and going after it despite obstacles and diversions. Perseverance is a powerful force that not only gets you what you want, but also gives you great satisfaction and enjoyment in the present. You humans get distracted too easily and often miss the enjoyment of the striving."

When I look back on my life, I see the wisdom in this. Most of my accomplishments were achieved through perseverance. Most of my satisfaction came from the effort.

Quotations

"Patience and perseverance have a magical effect before which difficulties disappear and obstacles vanish."
John Quincy Adams

"In the confrontation between the stream and the rock, the stream always wins. Not through strength, but through persistence."
Unknown

"Patience, persistence, and perspiration make an unbeatable combination for success."
Napoleon Hill

"Patience and tenacity of purpose are worth more than twice their weight of cleverness."
Thomas Henry Huxley

"Nothing in this world can take the place of persistence. Talent will not; nothing is more common than unsuccessful people with talent. Genius will not; unrewarded genius is almost a proverb. Education will not: the world is full of educated derelicts. Persistence and determination alone are omnipotent. The slogan 'press on' has solved and always will solve the problems of the human race."
Calvin Coolidge

40

Love yourself

Reilly licked his crotch. He does that a lot. "Why do you lick yourself so often?" I asked.

He stopped for a moment with a sly grin on his face. "Well, Bill, the obvious answer is because I can. But, it's more than that. I love being a dog and I love my body.

"It's very important to love yourself. If you don't, no one else will. Besides, for better or worse, that's who you are. No one else can ever be you and no one can take that away.

"Too many humans don't seem to like, much less love, themselves. They think they're not smart enough, not attractive enough, or not interesting enough. The reality is you are who you are … a wonderfully unique being in a wonderful world. Love yourself and your world will become a better, happier place."

This hit home for me. Don't we all waste precious time and energy wishing we could be different in one way or another?

Quotations

"You do not need to be loved, not at the cost of yourself. The single relationship that is truly central and crucial in a life is the relationship to the self. Of all the people you will know in a lifetime, you are the only one you will never lose."
Jo Coudert

"Self love is not opposed to the love of other people. You cannot really love yourself and do yourself a favor without doing people a favor, and visa versa."
Karl A. Menninger

"Love yourself – accept yourself – forgive yourself – and be good to yourself, because without you the rest of us are without a source of many wonderful things."
Leo F. Buscaglia

"If you can't accept yourself, than certainly no one else will."
Sasha Azevedo

"You yourself, as much as anybody in the entire universe deserve your love and affection."
Buddha

41

Life isn't fair

Reilly stopped for another drink of water and then continued, "You humans sometimes don't see the universe as it really is. You have this make believe vision of the world, as you would like it to be. In this fake world, you pretend that you'll always get what you deserve. You don't live in hope. You live in entitlement.

"We dogs, on the other hand, have no such illusions. Although we live in hope, we know the world isn't fair. It isn't unfair either. It just is. It's not what I deserve to get, it's what I do get. If I can get more, that's a good thing. If I can't get as much as I want, that's a good thing, too. I'm happy with whatever I can get. After all, I really don't have any choice in the matter. For the most part, neither do you."

Once again the little guy made sense. How many times have I ruined a moment, a day, or an experience by getting bent out of shape about what I thought I should have gotten?

Quotations

"Heaven goes by favor. If it went by merit, you would stay out and your dog would go in."
Mark Twain

"Life is never fair, and perhaps it is a good thing for most of us that it is not."
Oscar Wilde

"Life isn't fair. It's just fairer than death, that's all."
William Goldman

"If life was fair, Elvis would be alive and all the impersonators would be dead."
Johnny Carson

42

Play for keeps

Reilly gave me a whole body smile, butt swinging and tail wagging. "There is no happier creature in all of God's creation than I am when you let me off my lead to run around the backyard or to play with Cosmo or Gus. In five minutes, I will get more exercise than you get in a week. But it's not the exercise that's important. It's the fun. Whether I'm sleeping, eating, walking, or running, I have fun. You should, too.

"Meeting and play bowing to a new dog is like winning the lottery to me. A four-legged friend to smell and to play with is my vision of heaven on earth.

"I'm sure you're more interested in meeting the two-legged kind. Whenever you do, do your own play bow by making a real effort to play with them, to have fun with them. 'Play' doesn't mean only games and sports. It's having a happy time with others in whatever you're doing. It's doing the unexpected, laughing together, and having fun. You can play anywhere, even at work.

Play like you did when you were a child, Bill. Play like a dog! It will enrich your life and theirs."

Wow! It took me a while to get this but the point is so true. You can play at work. Play is not the activity but how it is enjoyed in the present moment.

Quotations

"The dog was created especially for children. He is the god of frolic."
Henry Ward Beecher

"A dog at play has the mind of a wise martial arts master, a mind capable of perfect focus."
Unknown

"Dogs motivate us to play, be affectionate, seek adventure, and be loyal."
Tom Hayden

"We do not stop playing because we grow old. We grow old because we stop playing."
Anonymous

"In every real man a child is hidden that wants to play."
Friedrich Nietzsche

"I think there's a little child in all of us and we all often forget to let the child out to play."
Donna A. Favors

"Live and work but do not forget to play, to have fun in life and really enjoy it."
Eileen Caddy

43

Have a soft mouth

"For a big dog, Reilly, I am often amazed at how gentle you are. I've seen what those jaws of yours can do. I haven't found a squeaky chew toy yet that you can't rip apart in minutes to get to the squeak mechanism inside. However, when I give you a treat, you never snap at it, but rather gently close your teeth around it and pull it away slowly. I've given treats to other dogs and have been surprised by their aggressive lunge and snap for the treat. Some of them have actually bitten my fingers."

"I can't speak for other dogs, Mr. Bill. Maybe they're aggressive because they're afraid. Maybe their masters aren't as gentle with them as you and Diane are with me. Maybe they've been mistreated. Or, maybe their masters teased them by offering treats and then pulling them away. Of course, they might just be really hungry.

"In my experience, gentleness achieves just as much, if not more, than aggressiveness. That's why I always tap you gently with a soft paw when I want to get your attention. That's how I get what I want because people and dogs respond more positively to gentleness. Besides, why should I aggressively lunge for something you are trying to give me? It makes no sense."

Whatever. He is a gentle soul.

Quotations

"The dog is a gentleman; I hope to go to his heaven, not man's."
Mark Twain

*"The most destructive element in the human mind
is fear. Fear creates aggressiveness."*
Dorothy Thompson

"Nothing is so strong as gentleness, nothing so gentle as real strength."
St. Francis de Sales

"In a gentle way you can shake the world."
Mahatma Gandhi

*"A gentle word, a kind look, a good natured smile can
work wonders and accomplish miracles."*
William Haslitt

"A gentle word opens an iron gate."
Bulgarian Proverb

44

Life's a treat to be shared

"You know how much I like treats?" asked Reilly. "Well, part of that is because of you. When you ask me, 'Want a treat?' I sense that you are happy.

"You see it's more than just the little chunk of food. You love me and you're happy to be giving me the treat. I'm happy you're happy and I'm happy to be getting the treat. We're both happy together at that moment in time. We're sharing food, sharing happiness, sharing one another, sharing love.

"I see all of life as a treat; the food, the water, the walks, the sleep, my family … everything. View life as a treat and share it with your friends and family and you'll be happy."

Reilly yawned, stood up and shook himself. With a shrug he said, "Well, that's about it, big guy. Those are my secrets to a happy life. Feel free to pass them on. Sorry if you were expecting something more, some ancient canine wisdom passed on by my forefathers. These are simple secrets because life is simple.

"To sum up: forget the past and don't wait for the future. Accept the present joyfully and live it fully. Love your family and friends, play a lot, and enjoy the life of Reilly."

What more can I add?

Quotations

"Learn from yesterday, live for today, hope for tomorrow."
Albert Einstein

"Very little is needed to make a happy life; it is all within yourself, in your way of thinking."
Marcus Aurelius

"The secret of health for both mind and body is not to mourn for the past, worry about the future, or anticipate troubles, but to live in the present moment wisely and earnestly."
Buddha

"Stop acting as if life is a rehearsal. Live this day as if it were your last. The past is over and gone. The future is not guaranteed."
Wayne Dyer

"Live this day as if it will be your last. Remember that you will only find 'tomorrow' on the calendars of fools. Forget yesterday's defeats and ignore the problems of tomorrow. This is it."
Og Mandino

"Carpe diem! Rejoice while you are alive; enjoy the day; live life to the fullest; make the most of what you have. It is later than you think."
Horace

Bill's Epilogue

How can you argue with Reilly's secrets? I began this project with at least some sense of human superiority. I thought I might discover a small kernel or two of wisdom from my canine companion. However, as he talked, more and more "kernels" poured forth from my friend and morphed into a coherent whole. I am now convinced we humans could benefit greatly by living like a dog in many, many ways. Reilly is truly my role model.

I'm sure you noticed similarities between some of Reilly's points. I know I did. I think that's because he comes at his core message of "being in the present" from different angles. The happiness he describes is sort of like the spokes on a wheel with the present moment being its hub.

For me, the difficulty lies not in the understanding or acceptance of these secrets; it's in their implementation. I may never be quite as happy as Reilly, but I'm sure gonna try. I hope you do, too. Be happy! Live like a dog!

Bill Curley

Quotation

"In order to really enjoy a dog, one doesn't merely try to train him to be semi human. The point of it is to open oneself to the possibility of becoming partly a dog."
Edward Hoagland,
Dogs and the Tug of Life

"I think dogs are the most amazing creatures; they give unconditional love. For me they are the role models for being alive."
Gilda Radner